CU00793437

Before Nicea

The Early Followers of Prophet Jesus

By
Abdul-Haq
&
Abdur-Rahmaan

URL: www.SalafiManhaj.com

E-mail: admin@salafimanhaj.com

Important Note:

The following document is an on-line book publishing of www.SalafiManhaj.com. This book was formatted and designed specifically for being placed on the Web and for its easy and convenient distribution. At the time of this e-book publishing, we are not aware of any other book similar to it, in terms of its content from its original source. Since this book was prepared for free on-line distribution we grant permission for it to be printed, disbursed, photocopied, reproduced and/or distributed by electronic means for the purpose of spreading its content and not for the purpose of gaining a profit, unless a specific request is sent to the publishers and permission is granted.

Published by : JamiahMedia
(www.JamiahMedia.net)

Researched & : AbdulHaq al-Ashanti &
Compiled by   Abdur-Rahmaan Bowes

Printed & : Impeks
Bound by   020 8808 6111

ISBN 0-9551099-0-6

Contents

Introduction [1]

Whilst seeking the truth, the honest investigator wants facts and this short work is intended for the sincere few who seek to know the original belief of the people that followed the teachings of Jesus, *peace be upon him.*

Before Nicea should not be viewed as 'Muslim propaganda' or bias, rather as a honest look at the evidence that qualified scholars have provided. This work also wants to move away from relying on the bible and blindly quoting from it in order to prove the true teachings of Jesus. Even though there is obviously some truth in the gospels, it is not the pure *Injeel* that is mentioned in the Qur'aan as being given to Jesus.

In assessing the comparisons between early Christianity and Islaam, the facts have been made accessible to the reader and presented in a manner that does not wish to antagonize. It is for the readers to make up their own minds and come to a conclusion about the evidence presented.

Conducted over the last three hundred years, such research is not a new phenomena. John Toland for example had written his book *The Nazarenes* in 1718 wherein he had already noticed the similar beliefs and practices of the early followers of Jesus and Muslims. Furthermore, John Biddle wrote *The True Opinion Concerning the Holy Trinity (Twelve Arguments)* in 1653, Joseph Priestly wrote eight books including *A General History of the Church,*

---

[1] *Before Nicea* was originally completed in 1998 by Paul Addae and Tim Bowes (Abdul-Haq and Abdur-Rahmaan) during their studies at the *School of Oriental and African Studies, University of London.* A version is also available from the *Da'wah* section at www.salafimanhaj.com

published in 1802 and *A History of the Corruption of Christianity*, published in 1871. A.C. MacGiffert wrote *A History of Christianity in the Apostolic Age* published in 1897, *The Apostles Creed* published in 1902 and *The God of the Early Christians* in 1924.

The discovery of the *Codex Sinaiticus*, the earliest almost complete manuscript (fourth century), brought with it more evidence for scholars to utilize. Using both these older sources and the recent research based upon the discoveries of early Christian manuscripts the reader will be supplied with that which is accepted as sound.

During conversations whilst compiling this work, it was noted that many evangelical Christians would argue that the Christian scholars quoted in this work for example are *'not really Christian.'* One of the *'Hyde Park Speakers Corner Christian Fellowship'* [2] even went so far as to say that there is not a single theologian who could be called a Christian, because he felt that theology is an enemy of Christianity. It is certainly true that most theologians do not understand the Bible to be 'divine revelation,' rather a combination of inspiration, commentary and interpretation. In many cases, these theologians will say that it was Jesus himself who was the 'divine revelation' and will feel perfectly free to reject the idea that the Bible is unadulterated.

Therefore, it is understandable that Christians who believe in the Bible as an uncorrupted whole, become hostile to such scholars. Nevertheless, Christian evangelical disapproval of theologians is quite contradictory and unreasonable, because it was on the grounds of theology that 'Christian' doctrine grew and unreasonable, as most Christians would be grateful that theology 'explained' for them many aspects of their belief.

---

[2] This is a well known and peculiar group that comprises a broad range of fundamentalist Christian evangelists of the London area who are active in propagating evangelical Christianity at London's Hyde Park Speaker's Corner.

Most of the scholars whom we have quoted are, to the best of our knowledge, practicing Christians. For example James Dunn's book *Christology in the Making* is illustrative of this fact. While he says at one point that "there is no real evidence in the earliest Jesus tradition of what could fairly be called a consciousness of divinity," (page 60), he makes no attempt to apologize for his conviction in Trinitarian Christianity. It is simply the fact that he is a Christian. Likewise, the New Testament scholar, the late Michael Ramsey, was an Archbishop in the Anglican church. We are fully aware that some of the writers whom we have quoted from are Christians so people should accept their dedicated research.

We note also Heikki Räisänen, a Christian interested in Christian-Muslim dialogue, who writes "Today it is clear to New testament scholarship that there is hardly anything in the New Testament even remotely like the doctrine of the Trinity. This realization may in itself be a fresh starting point for a dialogue." [3]

We are not going to judge whether they are *really* Christian or not, nor should an unqualified and emotional evangelical Christian make such judgments. We have put this booklet together simply as a basis of research for the sincere investigator.

Most of the writing of these historians, researchers and scholars is well referenced and we have been careful, when quoting from more controversial sources, to ensure that they have given references as evidence of authenticity. For example, we discovered in *The Holy Blood and the Holy Grail*, by Lincoln, Baigent and Leigh (1982), a reference to a text in the *Nag Hammadi Scrolls*. While it is obvious that their book is overflowing with unacceptable conjecture, it was possible to make further investigations to discover that the text in question within the *Nag Hammadi Scrolls* does indeed exist.

---

[3] Heikki Räisänen, *The Portrait of Jesus in the Qur'an*, 1980, p.127

There are a number of sources which we have used whose books contain subjective and objective opinions. In such cases we have largely ignored their conjecture and theories and have only quoted from that which may be called established fact. For example, we have made reference to *The Five Gospels* (1993) by the *'Jesus Seminar.'* While the main body of their work is concerned with demythologizing the gospels and using a consensus of 'opinion' to determine the authenticity of the sayings of Jesus, which may be unacceptable, we have quoted from their book that which is attested to by historical evidence.

More importantly, Allaah mentions in the Qur'aan

> ❴They follow only conjecture and what their souls desire – even though there has already come down to them guidance from their Lord ❵   *{an-Najm (53): 23}*

In some cases, the sources that we have used may be unsympathetic towards Islaam, but what is most striking is to discover that parallels do exist between the early Christianity of these studies and Islam. Often this appears to be unapparent to the writers, but on occasions, some are quite ready to admit this parallel. For example, Hans Küng et al write that the, **"traditional and historical parallels between Judaic-Christianity and Islam are inescapable."** [4]

Hans-Joachim Schoeps[5] comes to a similar conclusion as does Professor Eisenman. Indeed, as we stated earlier, the knowledge of the similarities between early Christianity and Islam has been studied thoroughly. Writers such as Francis David (1510-1579), Michael Servetus (1511-1553), Adam

---

[4] Christianity and the World Religions – Paths of Dialogue with Islam, Hinduism & Buddhism, 1986, p. 124
[5] Theology and History in Jewish Christianity, 1949, p. 342

Neuser (circa 1570) and John Toland (in 1718) were describing such parallels several hundred years ago! [6]

Obviously we are writing as Muslims, but we have tried our best not to present the wrong information. Having gone through the process of 'coming to Islaam' ourselves, we understand the difficulties in knowing exactly *who* is telling the truth. When speaking with Christians prior to beginning this compilation of quotations, we were interested that few were aware of the historical material about the early followers of Jesus, as studies by many scholars, historians and theologians, and the origins and development of Christianity.

We have therefore sifted through the speculation of many books and articles about early Christianity, to present the reader with factual evidence, as it stands in light of Islaam. It will consequently be apparent that while Christianity may be a religion *about* Jesus, it was not necessarily the religion *of* Jesus *(peace be upon him)*. Thus we invite the reader to sincerely reflect and by the will of Allaah, they will come to understand and *Inshaa'Allaah* know the truth.

---

[6] See Adrian Reland, *Treatises Concerning the Mahametons*, (18th century), pp. 215-22; also W.C Garnett, *Francis David – Founder of Unitarianism* (1914); R.H. Bainton, *The Hunted Heretic* (1953); D.B. Parke, *The Epic of Unitarainism* (1957), pp. 5-6

The Crucifixion

❝They said (in boast), "We have killed the Messiah, Jesus the son of Mary, the Messenger of Allaah" – But they did not kill him, nor did they crucify him; but (another) was made to resemble him to them. And indeed, those who differ over it are in doubt about it. They have no knowledge of it and follow only conjecture. And they did not kill him, being certain (of his identity)❞
{an-Nisaa (4): 157}

The Qur'aanic statement that Jesus was neither slain nor crucified and that another was killed whom they assumed was Jesus, stands very much in favour of the divine origin of the Qur'aan. Many argue that had Muhammad been a forger, the crucifixion would be the last detail he would 'change.' However, further study reveals that Christians during the pre-Islamic era followed just as diverse doctrines as they do today. Amongst these beliefs were that Jesus was not crucified and many early Christian sects denied that the crucifixion even occurred. This begs the question as to why they denied the crucifixion of Jesus?

H.M. Gwatkin in *Early Church History* states **"The stumbling block of the age of early Christianity was not so much Jesus' divinity, but his crucifixion."** [7]

Some of the first groups that followed the way of Jesus and also several other historical sources other than the Qur'aan confirm that Jesus did not die on the cross. John Toland in his work *The Nazarenes* mentions that

---

[7] Volume 1, p.11

Plotinus who lived in the 4th century stated that he had read a book called *The Journeys of the Apostles* which related traditions of Peter, John, Andrew, Thomas and Paul. Among other things, the book stated that Jesus was not crucified, but rather another in his place, and therefore Jesus and the apostles had laughed at those who believed Jesus had died on the cross.[8] Also similar to the belief of Basileides and his followers/students who were known as the *Basildians*.[9]

H. Lincoln, Michael Baigent and Richard Leigh in their controversial and critically acclaimed *The Holy Blood and the Holy Grail*[10] mention a historical text, The *Nag Hammadi Scrolls*[11] and state that these manuscripts contain a manuscript entitled 'The Treaties of Seth.' Here it is mentioned that Jesus was not crucified even though a crucifixion did take place, Simon of Cyrene was the victim and not Jesus.

J. Stevenson, a *Cambridge University* lecturer of divinity, notes that Irenaeus describes the teachings of Basileides. While Basileides and his followers believed that Jesus was the god of the Jews and other strange things about the creation of the universe, with regards to the crucifixion of Jesus they said "He appeared, then, on earth as a man, to the nations of these powers, and wrought miracles. **Wherefore he did not himself suffer death, but a certain Simon of Cyrene, being compelled, bore the cross in his stead. Simon was transfigured by him, so that he might be thought to be Jesus, and was crucified, through ignorance and error.**" [12]

---

[8] John Toland, *The Nazarenes* (1718), p.18 - It can be found at the *British Library*

[9] J. Stevenson (ed.), *A New Eusebius - Documents Illustrative of the History of the Church to AD 337* (London: SPCK, 1957), p.82

[10] (1982), p.409

[11] Discovered in December 1945 in the town of Nag Hammadi in the cliffs that skirt the Nile through Upper Egypt by an Egyptian farmer named Muhammad 'Ali. The scrolls were studied by the French scholar and antiquities dealer Jean Doresse who was working in Cairo for an antiquities dealer

[12] *A New Eusebius*, pp 81-82

Cerinthus[13], a contemporary of Peter, Paul and John, also denied that Christ died on the cross and that Christ did not suffer because he was a spiritual being.[14] The *'Carpocratians'* also believed that Jesus did not die on the cross but another person that resembled him.

Also the early community of Christians called the *'Docetae,'* held that Jesus never had a real physical body, only an apparent or illusory body. Therefore, the crucifixion was *apparent*, not real.[15]

In the *Gospel of Mark* (15: 21), the Greek word translated as *'to carry,'* where Simon of Cyrene *'carried'* the cross, should actually be translated as *'to bare.'* There are some who argue that this indicates that Simon of Cyrene *bore* the cross and was crucified not Jesus in fact. This of course puts it in agreement with the beliefs of the other early groups that followed the way of Jesus. Simon of Cyrene is not mentioned anywhere else in Biblical tradition and a study of Greek is therefore necessary.

All of these notions of the crucifixion differ from the 'orthodox' Christian understanding, illustrating that there were indeed varied beliefs amongst the early followers of Jesus. These would later be deemed as 'heretics,' by 'orthodox' Christians with beliefs much further away from the teachings, belief and practice of Jesus, *peace be upon him*.

Another interesting piece of evidence from the *Gospel of Mark*, chapter 15, is the passage that informs of Pontious Pilate, finding no fault with Jesus, saw fit to release him. **"Following a Passover custom unknown outside the gospels, Pilate offered to free a Jewish prisoner and suggested Jesus, but the crowd...demanded that Pilate release Barabbas and crucify Jesus."**[16]

---

[13] His followers were known as the *'Cerinthians'*

[14] *A New Eusebius*, p 96

[15] Leonard George, *Crimes of Perception - An Encyclopedia of Heresies and Heretics* (Paragon House: 1995) and *A New Eusebius*, pp. 47-48, 96, 101-102 and 152

[16] Bruce Metzger and Michael D. Coogan (eds.), *The Oxford Companion to the Bible* (Oxford University Press: 1993), p.74

In the earliest Greek manuscripts, Barabbas was referred to as *'Jesus Barabbas.'* This is particularly interesting as Gregory Shaw writes: "Outside the Gospels nothing is known of Barabbas. His name is Aramaic and means *"son of the father" (*Abba)*, ironically denoting the status given exclusively to Jesus."[17]

From this then, it is unclear as to who was actually crucified, since both characters had exactly the same name! In fact, the one who was released could more strongly be identified with the one whom Christians insist was crucified. As if this was not enough, it would otherwise indicate that *"son of the father"* was *not* an exclusive title, as some Christians claim with reference to the word *'Abba.'*

There has been the argument that because the crucifixion is mentioned by the historians Josephus and Tacitus this therefore proves that Jesus was crucified. However, it should be noted that Josephus and Tacitus merely state that a pious worshiper of God called Jesus lived, taught and was later crucified. Their accounts are not eye-witness accounts but most probably hearsay accounts due to the massive uproar in the area at the time from the impact of Jesus with the Jews and Romans. It is in fact the case that Josephus was only born circa 38 CE indicating that he was an historian and not an eye witness. Geza Vermes of Oxford University has shown that the works of Josephus have been altered by the later Christians who inserted their own version of events into the writings of Josephus.

[17] ibid

Early Christianity

❲Oh you who have believe! Be the helpers of Allaah as said Jesus Son of Mary to the disciples, "who are my helpers (in the cause) of Allaah?" The disciples said "we are Allaah's helpers." Then a group of the children of Israel believed and a group disbelieved. So we gave power to those who believed against their enemies, and they became the victorious.❳ *{as-Saff (61): 14}*

At his ascension, Jesus, *peace be upon him*, left behind a multitude of followers relying on what he had taught them for the worship of God.[18] According to the Qur'aan, he never said anything about God or himself which he had no right to say. He was a man and a Prophet who told his followers to worship One God, as Muslims. However, to the Christians, all of this is of no consequence for they do not consider the Qur'aan to be the word of God. Therefore, the objective of this section is to present the information of researchers on this subject.

Around 90 CE, the *Shepard of Hermas* was considered to be a book of revelation by the church, according to EJ Goodspeed and is one of two books found in the *Codex Sinaiticus*, which have not been included in the modern Bible.[19] In it are twelve commandments and the first is: "**believe that God is One and that He created all things and organized them,**

---

[18] The Unitarian concept of God and the prophetic human nature of Jesus, was held by many early communities basing their way of life on the teachings of Jesus, such as the *Ebionites*, the *Nazarenes*, the *Cerinthians*, the *Basilidians*, the *Carpocratians*, the *Hypsistarians*, the *Symmachians* and the *Elkesaites*.

[19] *The Apostolic Fathers* (1950)

and out of what did not exist made all things to be, and He contains all things but Alone is Himself uncontained. Trust Him therefore and fear Him, and, fearing Him, be self-controlled. Keep this command and you will cast away from yourself all wickedness, put on every virtue of uprightness, and you will live to God if you keep this commandment."

Here God is One and He is uncontained, comparatively, the Anglican affirmation of faith (the *Nicene Creed*) however goes: "I believe in One God, the father almighty, Maker of the heaven and earth, and of all things visible and invisible; and in one Lord Jesus Christ, the only-begotten Son of God, begotten of his father before all worlds, God of God, Light of Light, very God of very God, begotten, not made, being of one substance with the Father, by whom all things were made...And I believe in the Holy Ghost, the Lord, the Giver of Life, who proceedeth from the Father and the Son, who with the Father and the Son together is worshipped and glorified, who spoke by Prophets..."[20]

According to Theodore Zahn in *Articles of the Apostolic Creed*[21] until around 250 CE the article of faith was simply, "I believe in God, the Almighty," which today is only one element of the Anglican creed. J.R. Harris quoted Aristedes, an early Christian apologist as saying that **"the Christian worship in the beginning was more purely monotheistic than that even of the Jews."**[22]

During the early history of the Christian church there existed a prospering group called the *'Ebionites.'* On the origin of the term Robert Wilken says that this Hebrew word means *'poor persons'* and continues to explain that there is no evidence to support the claim of some Christian writers that it is derived from a person called *'Ebion,'* he highlights: **"The origin, history**

---

[20] Alternative Service Book, (1980)

[21] (1899), pp. 33-37

[22] J.R. Harris, *Celsus and Aristedes* (1921)

and distinct character of the *Ebionites* has been subject to intense
debate in recent years. It is possible that the *Ebionites* go back to the
earliest period of Christian history, where most Christians were Jews
and some continued to observe the Jewish law. If so, they would be
the earliest example of a Christian movement within Judaism that
was eventually left behind as Christianity adapted to the influx of
gentile converts. These Christians eventually became a distinct group
that, along with other groups (e.g. the *Gnostics*) was rejected as
heretical by the emerging 'great' church. They are sometimes
identified with the *Minim* (heretics) mentioned in the Talmud. The
Ebionites were Jews who accepted Jesus of Nazareth as the *Messiah*
(Christ) while continuing to maintain their identity as Jews. They
cultivated relations with Jews as well as Christians though they were
welcomed by neither. They followed the Jewish law, insisting on
circumcision, keeping the Sabbath and celebrating the Jewish
festivals (*Yom Kippur, Passover* etc.) and observing the dietary laws
(e.g. abstention from pork) and other Jewish customs. They
repudiated the apostle Paul because of his denigration of the Jewish
law. They saw Jesus as a prophet, an exceptional man in the line of
Jewish prophets (as described in Deuteronomy 18: 15) and denied
the virgin birth. They justified their way of life by appealing to the
example of Jesus' life. He was circumcised, observed the *Sabbath* and
celebrated the Jewish festivals, and taught that all the precepts of the
law should be observed. They celebrated *Easter* on the same day that
the Jews celebrated the *Passover*, and they held the city of Jerusalem
in high esteem."[23]

Furthermore, there were other Jewish Christian sects according to Wilken,
including the *Nazarenes*[24], the*Symmachians* and the *Elkesaites*. Because it is
difficult to distinguish one from another, he suggests that '*Ebionite*' may
have been used to characterize any form of Jewish Christianity which

---

[23] The Encyclopedia of Religions, p. 576
[24] They believed in the virgin birth and that Jesus was a Prophet and the Messiah of the
Jewish peoples

stressed observance of the law. The *Ebionites* had their own gospel and ancient writers, according to Wilken, mention three Jewish Christian gospels. Wilken writes: **"There was a resurgence of Jewish Christianity in the late fourth century, encouraged by Jewish messianism…after this period little is known about the *Ebionites*."**

According to *Compton's Encyclopedia* the early Jewish Christians were persecuted because they recognized that Jesus was the expected Messiah, while the Jewish authorities considered him as an imposter and traitor: "The early Christians were all Jews. They remained in Jerusalem and partook in the religious observances in the Temple. They differed from their fellow Jews only in that they believed that the Messiah had come. Had they kept quiet about their conviction, they might well have remained a sect within Judaism. However, they insisted on preaching to all who would listen that the Jesus whom the Jewish authorities had persecuted was the one Israel had long awaited. This preaching aroused great hostility on the part of religious leaders and the early Christians were persecuted…these Christians had no thought of venturing beyond the confines of Israel with their message."[25]

The Unitarian concept of God and the prophetic human nature of Jesus, was held by many early communities basing their way of life on the teachings of Jesus, such as the *Ebionites*, the *Nazarenes*, the *Cerinthians*, the *Basilidians*, the *Carpocratians*, the *Hypsistarians*, the *Symmachians* and the *Elkesaites*.

Trinitarian Christians point out that these groups have 'always been seen as heretical by the early Church,' by this they mean the *prevailing* Church without attempting to establish whether that Church followed authentic teachings. To repeat Wilken, the *Ebionites* for example were **"eventually left behind as Christianity adapted to the influx of gentile converts.**

---

[25] Compton's Encyclopedia, *'Christianity,'* (CD – ROM Home Library, 1997)

These Christians eventually became a distinct group that, along with other groups (e.g. the *Gnostics*) was rejected as heretical by the emerging 'great' church."[26]

This shows that the so called '*heretical*' church was rejected by an '*emerging*' Christianity. In other words, the earlier followers of Jesus' teachings were to be condemned by later followers of an adopted faith.

In *Theology and History of Jewish Christianity,* Hans-Joachim Schoeps taking up the research of Harnack and Schlatter and completing it with studies by C. Clemen, T. Andrae and H.H. Schaeder comes to the following broadly substantiated conclusion: "Though it may not be possible to establish exact proof of the connection, the indirect dependence of Muhammad on sectarian Jewish Christianity is beyond any doubt. This leaves us with a paradox of truly world historical dimensions: the fact while Jewish Christianity in the Church came to grief (disappeared) it was preserved in Islam and, with regard to some of its driving impulses at least, it has lasted till our own time."[27]

Hans Küng et al. note that "the traditional and historical parallels between early Judaic-Christianity and Islam are inescapable."[28]

John Toland writing in 1718 concluded: "Since the *Nazarenes,* or *Ebionites,* are by all the Church historians unanimously acknowledged to have been the first Christians, or those who believed him from amongst the Jews, who were his own people and apostles, with which he lived and died and witnessed his actions, considering this, I say how was it possible for them to be the first of all others (for they were made to be the first heretics), who should form wrong conceptions of the doctrines and designs of Jesus? And how did the

---

[26] The Encyclopedia of Religions, p. 576
[27] Hans-Joachim Schoeps, Theology and History of Jewish Christianity (1949), p.342
[28] Hans Küng (ed.), Christianity and the World Religions – Paths of Dialogue with Islam, Hinduism and Buddhism (1986), p.24

Gentiles, who only believed in Jesus after his death from the preaching and information of people that never knew Jesus, have truer notions of doctrine and Jesus, or whence could they have their information but from the believing Jews."[29]

---

[29] John Toland, *The Nazarenes* (1718), p.73-76 – The book can be found at the *British Library*

Paul

❴Indeed, those who conceal what Allaah has sent down of the Book and exchange it for a small price – they will swallow nothing but the fire. Allaah will not speak to them on the Day of Resurrection, nor will He purify them; and they will have a painful punishment❵ {*Baqarah (2): 174*}

A.N. Wilson noted that Jesus had no intention of founding a new faith and that he was a Jew with a mission aimed at the Jewish inhabitants of Palestine.[30] This research therefore confirms Islaam's position of Jesus as a Prophet and Messiah for the Jews. Heinz Zahrnt calls Paul **"the corrupter of the Gospel of Jesus."**[31]

The writer Michael H. Hart in his ranking of the most influential people in human history put Paul at number two, after Muhammad, Jesus comes in at number three.[32] Verde describes Paul as "the second founder of Christianity," thus due to Paul **"the discontinuity between the historical Jesus and the Christ of the Church became so great that any unity between them is scarcely recognizable."**[33]

Groliers Encyclopedia records that: "By the middle of the first century, missionaries were spreading the new religion of Christianity among the peoples of Egypt, Syria, Anatolia, Greece and Italy. Chief among these was

---

[30] A.N. Wilson, Paul – *The Mind of the Apostle*, 1997
[31] Johannes Lehman, *The Jesus Report*, p.126
[32] Michael H. Hart, The 100 – *A Ranking of the Most Influential Persons in History*, 1978
[33] *The Jesus Report*, p.128

Saint Paul, who laid the foundations of Christian theology and played a key role in the transformation of Christianity from a Jewish sect to a world religion. **The original Christians, being Jews, observed the dietary and ritualistic laws of the Torah** and required non-Jewish converts to do the same. **Paul and others favoured eliminating obligation, thus making Christianity more attractive to Gentiles.**"

Comptons Encyclopedia informs: "Yet **these (first) Christians had no thought of venturing beyond the confines of Israel with their message. It was only with the appearance of a man named Saul of Tarsus (Paul) that the assembly of believers enlarged its horizons to include the whole world. Saul, a strict Jew, was a persecutor of the Church.** He was, nevertheless converted, and, after changing his name to 'Paul,' began what is called the 'mission to the gentiles.' It was this man who, more than any other, pulled the Church out from the Temple and Synagogue and set it apart as a separate institution. **But the separation was, for Paul, more than a physical one. It was also doctrinal.** Christians, he asserted, did not have to become Jews. They were not subject to all the rites, rituals, and laws of Israel's religion. This, perhaps more than any other factor, aroused the intense hostility of the Jews and led to a definitive separation of the two camps. The books of the New testament, particularly the writings of Paul, contain the early Church's testimonies about who Jesus was and what his life meant."

Misha'al al-Kadhi in his book *What Did Jesus Really Say?* has noted that Jesus *(peace be upon him)*, according to the testimony of the gospels, commanded mankind to strictly observe the religion of Moses until the end of time (Matthew 5: 18) and that **"unless you show yourselves far better than the scribes and Pharisees, you can never enter the kingdom of Heaven"** (5: 20). Further, Jesus is said to have told his followers that observing the religion and laws given to Moses and the selling of their belongings would make them achieve entry into heaven (Luke 18: 18-22). After the departure of Jesus, Paul, by his own admission savagely persecuted countless Christians (Galatians 1: 13-15; Acts 8; 1-3); (Acts 9: 1-2; Acts 22:4). Paul also 'stood by approving' as the Apostle Stephen was stoned to death (Acts 22:20). Paul becomes convinced that he has received 'visions' and is 'saved' (Acts 22: 6-12; Acts 9: 3-10), even though Paul is not exactly sure exactly of what he saw in these 'visions' he knows that they contained **"unspeakable words that are unlawful to utter,"** (2 Corinthians 12: 1-5).[34] Paul then claims that the 'person' in these visions was Jesus and that he was given the teachings of Christianity and no one else had access to this gospel except Paul (Galatians 11: 12), not even the Apostles who lived, preached, ate and drank with Jesus for many years. Paul stipulates that he is free to do anything and that he will not let anything make free with him (1 Corinthians 6: 12) and that he shall do whatever it takes to get people to follow him, no matter what that might entail and even if it involves "behaving outside the law" (1 Corinthians 9: 20-22). Paul, who never met Jesus, arrogantly boasts of how he is better than the Apostles, who were eyewitnesses, companions and first-hand true disciples of Jesus, by stating that "by the grace of God and in my labours I have outdone them all" (1 Corinthians 15: 10). Further, Paul, with clearly arrogant expressions which makes it obvious that he deviated from the true teachings of Jesus who would not and did not encourage this kind of conceited talk, regards the Apostles as "lacking principles," "playing false" and having "conduct that did not square up to the true gospel" (Galatians 2: 13-14).

Dr A. Meyer, Professor of Theology at *Zurich University* stated in the book *Jesus or Paul*: "If by 'Christianity' we understand faith in Jesus Christ as the heavenly son of God, who did not belong to Earthly humanity, but who lived in the divine likeness and glory, who came down from heaven to earth, who entered humanity and took upon himself a human form through a virgin, that he might make propitiation for men's sins by his own blood on the cross, who was then awakened from death and raised to God as the Lord of his own people, who believe in him, who hears their prayers, guards and leads them, who shall come again to judge the world, who will cast

---

[34] It should be noted that the *Ebionites* and the *Nazarenes* argued that Paul had in fact received demonic hallucinations whist others accused Paul of being a spy for the Romans posing as a follower of Jesus (*The Jesus Report*, p.123).

down all the foes of God, and will bring his people with him unto the house of heavenly light so that they may become like his glorified body – **if this is Christianity, the such a Christianity was founded by Paul and not by Jesus.**"[35]

The impact of Paul in laying the foundations of Christianity has further been analysed by Hyam Maccoby in *The Mythmaker – Paul and the Invention of Christianity* [36] and by David Wenham in *Paul – Follower of Jesus or Founder of Christianity*.[37]

[35] Meyer, *Jesus or Paul*, p.122
[36] New York: Harper and Row, 1987
[37] Eerdmans, 1995

Is Jesus God?

Hasting in *The Dictionary of the Bible* says: "It is doubtful whether Jesus used the expression 'Son of god' to refer to himself."

Adrian Thatcher wrote: "There is scarcely a single competent New Testament scholar who is prepared to defend the view that the four instances of the absolute use of "I am" in John, or indeed most of the other uses, can be historically attributed to Jesus." [38]

David Brown stated that: "**There is good evidence to suggest that Jesus never saw himself as a suitable object of worship,**" it is "impossible to base any claim for Christ's divinity on his consciousness once we abandon the traditional portrait as reflected in a literal understanding of St. John's Gospel."[39] But, he says, "It is incoherent to suppose that a human mind could be conscious of its own divinity." [40]

The late Archbishop and New Testament scholar, Michael Ramsey, wrote: "**Jesus did not claim deity for himself.**" [41] He also stated: "The title *'Son of God'* need not of itself be of high significance, for in Jewish circles it might mean no more than the Messiah or indeed the whole Israelite nation, and in popular Hellenism there were many sons of God, meaning inspired holy men." [42]

---

[38] Adrian Thatcher, *Truly a Person, Truly God* (London: SPCK, 1990) p.77
[39] David Brown, *The Divine Trinity* (1985) p. 108
[40] ibid. p. 106
[41] Michael Ramsey, *Jesus and the Living Past* (1980) p. 39
[42] ibid. p. 43

In ancient Hebrew and Aramaic, to be known as 'son of God' did not carry a literal meaning and merely emphasized that such a person was a servant of God. In the Arabic language for example there is a similar device utilised in which people are referred to as being the *"father of..."* or the *"mother of...."*

In the Bible, Israel (Prophet Jacob) is referred to being the 'son of God' (Exodus 4:22-23), Prophet Soloman is called the 'son of God' (2 Samuel 8:13-14), God also promises to make David 'His son.' In Jeremiah 31:9: "...for I am a father to Israel and Ephraim is my first-born." In the Book of Job (1:6), angels are referred to as "sons of God," the author of the Gospel according to Luke listed Jesus' ancestors back to Adam and wrote "the son of Enos, the son of Seth, the son of Adam, the son of God" (Luke 3:38). Jesus refers to himself as the "son of Man" in the Bible (e.g. Luke 9:22) and never at all in the Bible does he refer to himself as being the "son of God."

Sulayman Mufassir notes that in the New Testament *Book of Acts*, there are several speeches of the early disciples of Jesus which date from the year 33 CE. In of such discourses, Jesus is referred to specifically as *andra apo tou theou* ("a man from God"), Acts 2:22. Not once do these early confessions of faith use the expression *wios tou theou* ("son of God") but they do speak several times of Jesus as being God's servant and prophet (Acts 3:13, 22, 23, 26). These speeches therefore reflect the actual early belief and terminology of the disciples before their beliefs came under the influence of Roman religion and Greek philosophy. **"They reflect a tradition which is older than that used by the Four Gospels, in which Jesus is not invested with godship or divine sonship."** [43]

---

[43] Sulayman Shahid Mufassir, *Biblical Studies From a Muslim Perspective* (Washington: The Islamic Center, 1973), p.12

James Barr argues that the expression *abba*, commonly used to illustrate Jesus' 'divine sonship,' did not have the intimate sense that is often attributed to it, but simply meant 'father.'[44]

James Dunn mentions both arguments, for and against, for the nature of the use of *'Abba.'* Dunn also says: **"There is no real evidence in the earliest Jesus traditions of what could fairly be called a consciousness of divinity."**[45]

Brian Hebblewaite admits, **"It is no longer possible to defend the divinity of Jesus by reference to the claims of Jesus."**[46]

Sanders writes: "The oft-repeated claim that Jesus "put himself in the place of God" is overdone. He is often said to have done so in forgiving sins, but we must note that he only pronounced forgiveness, which is not the prerogative of God, but of the priesthood."[47]

Professor John Hick noted: **"For to say, without explanation, that the historical Jesus of Nazareth was also God is as devoid of meaning...that Jesus was God the Son incarnate is not literally true, since it has no literal meaning, but it an application to Jesus of a mythical concept whose function is analogous to that of the notion of divine sonship ascribed in ancient world to a king."**[48]

---

[44] James Barr, *'Abba, Father'* in *Theology Journal* – Vol. 91, no. 741; 1988

[45] James Dunn, Christology in the Makling, p.60

[46] Brian Hebblewaite, *The Incarnation* (1987), p. 74

[47] Sanders, *Jesus and Judaism* (1985), p.240

[48] John Hick, *The Myth of God Incarnate* (London: SCM Press, 1977), p.178

The Trinity

⟨O People of the scripture, do not commit excess in your religion (by attributing divine qualities to the creations of Allaah and worshiping them excessively or say about Allaah except the truth). The Messiah, Jesus, the son of Mary, was but a messenger of Allaah and His word which he directed to Mary, and a soul (created by a command) from Him. So believe in Allaah and His messengers. Do not say "Three," desist – it will be better for you. Indeed, Allaah is One God, glory be to Him, exalted is He above having a son. To Him belong all things in the heavens and on the earth. And sufficient is Allaah as a Disposer of affairs⟩ {an-Nisaa: 171}

For the majority of Christians today, the trinity is a key concept, but for the early followers of Jesus it was unheard of. *The New Catholic Encyclopedia*, officially approved by the Catholic Church, explains that the concept of the Trinity was introduced into Christianity in the fourth century: "There is the recognition on the part of exegetes and biblical theologians, including a constantly growing number of Roman Catholics, that one should not speak of Trinitarianism in the New Testament without serious qualification. There is also the closely parallel recognition on the part of historians of dogma and systematic theologians that when one does speak of an unqualified Trinitarianism, one has moved from the period of Christian origins to, say, the last quadrant of the 4th century. **It was only then that what might be called the definitive Trinitarian dogma 'One God in three persons' became thoroughly assimilated into Christian life and thought...it was the product of three centuries of doctrinal development.**"[49]

---

[49] *The New Catholic Encyclopedia* – Volume 14, p.295

The Oxford Companion to the Bible which has entries from over two hundred and sixty scholars and academics from leading biblical institutes and universities in America and Europe states: "Because the Trinity is such an important part of later Christian doctrine, it is striking that the term does not appear in the New Testament. Likewise, the developed concept of three co-equal partners in the Godhead found in later creedal formulations cannot be clearly detected within the confines of the canon."[50]

John McKenzie in *The Dictionary of the Bible* notes :
"The Trinity of God is defined by the Church as the belief that in God is three persons who subsist in one nature. That belief as so defined was reached only in the 4th and 5th centuries AD and hence is not explicitly and formally a biblical belief."[51]

David Lyle Jeffrey, writing in the *Dictionary of Biblical Tradition in English Literature* mention: "According to orthodox Christian doctrine, God is one nature in three persons: Father, Son and Holy Spirit. No one of them precedes or created the others or stands above them in power or dignity. In precise theological terms, they are one in substance (or essence), coeternal and co-equal. The doctrine so stated does not appear in scripture, the orthodox doctrine of the Trinity was hammered out gradually over a period of three centuries or more. Unsurprisingly, perhaps, the coeternity and coequality of the divine persons remained a matter of theological dispute, and are thus frequently discussed in the context of heresy. In 381 the bishops convened again at Constantinople and set forth the orthodox doctrine in its final form."[52]

---

[50] Bruce Metzger and Michael D. Coogan (eds.), *The Oxford Companion to the Bible* (Oxford University Press, 1993) pp. 782-783

[51] John McKenzie, The Dictionary of the Bible, p899

[52] David Lyle Jeffrey, Dictionary of Biblical Tradition in English Literature, p.785

Bernard Lohse admits "it is true that particularly in reference to the beginnings of the doctrine of the trinity there is still much uncertainty...as far as the New Testament is concerned, one does not find in it an actual doctrine of the trinity." [53]

Bernard Piault in *The 20th Century Encyclopedia of Catholicism* noted: "It is a good thing to examine the revelation that God made to the Jewish people in the Old Testament. We shall not find in it a lesson on the trinity, there is none." [54]

F.J. Wilken, the Australian Baptist, wrote in *Christadelphianism*: "In the Old Testament, the Unity of God, was clearly affirmed. The Jewish creed, repeated in every synagogue today was 'Hear, O Israel, the Lord our God is One Lord (Deut. 6:4). This was the faith of the first Christians, so Paul writes, 'There is one god and Father of all, Who is above all and through all and in you all'" (Eph. 4:6). But gradually some addition or modification of this creed was found necessary." [55]

Regarding textual evidence of the Trinity, *The Interpreter's Dictionary of the Bible* highlights: "The text about the three heavenly witnesses (1 John 5: 7 *KJV*) is not an authentic part of the New Testament." [56]

"1 John 5: 7 in the King James Version reads: 'There are three that bear record in heaven, the father, the Word and the Holy Ghost, and these three are one' but this is an interpolation of which there is no trace before the late fourth century." [57]

---

[53] Bernard Lohse, A Short History of Christian Doctrine, 1966, p.39
[54] Bernard Piault, 'What is the Trinity' in 20th Century Encyclopedia of Catholicism, Vol. 20
[55] F.J. Wilken, Christadelphianism
[56] The Interpreter's Dictionary of the Bible – Volume 4, p.711
[57] ibid. p. 871

The *Eerdmans Bible Dictionary* reports: "1 John 5: 7 in the *Textus Receptus* (represented in the King James Version) makes it appear that John had arrived at the doctrine of the Trinity in explicit form ('the Father, the Son and the Holy Ghost'), but **this text is clearly an interpolation since no genuine Greek manuscript contains it.**" [58]

Shirley C. Guthrie mentioned: "**The Bible does not teach the doctrine of the trinity. Neither the word trinity itself, nor such language as one in three, three in one, one essence or substance or three persons, is biblical language. The language of the doctrine is the language of the ancient Church, taken not from the bible but from classical Greek philosophy.**" [59]

Edward Gibbon also recognized that this was a fabrication and while this fact is now widely accepted as fact and has been removed from most translations of the Bible, such acceptance took time. Richard Porson defended Gibbon, later publishing devastatingly conclusive proof that the verse was first inserted by the Church into the Bible at the end of the fourth century. Regarding his finding, Porson concluded: "His structures are founded in argument, enriched with learning, and enlivened with wit, and his adversary neither deserves nor finds any quarter at his hands. **The evidence of the three heavenly witnesses would now be rejected in any court of justice; but prejudice is blind, authority is deaf, and our vulgar bibles will ever be polluted by this spurious text.**" [60]

---

[58] The Eerdmans Bible Dictionary, p. 1020

[59] Shirley C. Guthrie, *Christian Doctrine*, p.92

[60] James Bentley, *Secrets of Mount Sinai*, pp.30-33

The Bible: Its Alteration, Compilation and Translation

《Woe (destruction) to those who write the "scripture" with their own hands, then say "This is from Allaah," in order to exchange it for a small price. Woe (destruction) to them for what their own hands have written and woe (destruction) to them for what they earn》 {Baqarah: 79}

Martin Kahler notes "We do not possess any sources for a 'life of Jesus' which a historian can accept as reliable and adequate. I repeat: we have no sources for a biography of Jesus of Nazareth which measure up to the standards of contemporary historical science." [61]

Kenneth Cragg states about the New Testament, "There is condensation and editing, there is choice production and witness. The Gospels have come through the mind of the church behind the authors. They represent experience and history." [62]

Similarly, Dr Von Tishendorf, one of the most resolute conservative defenders of the Trinity, admitted that the New Testament had "in many passages undergone such serious modification of meaning as to leave us in painful uncertainty as to what the Apostles had actually written." [63]

---

[61] Martin Kahler, The So-Called Historical Jesus and the Historic Biblical Christ,

[62] Kenneth Cragg, The Call of the Minaret, p.277

[63] James Bentley, Secrets of Mount Sinai, p.117

The purpose of this section is to bring together the facts about the Bible, as presented by many Christian scholars. It is interesting that the author of the Old Testament book, Jeremiah, recognized the same facts all those many years ago: "How can you say, "We are wise, we have the law of the Lord," when scribes with their lying pens have falsified it? The wise are put to shame; they are dismayed and entrapped. They have spurned the word of the Lord, so what sort of wisdom is theirs?" [64]

Alteration and Transmission of the Bible
Theologians recognize that the Bible contains many contradictions and prefer not to explain them away as some do. Simply, they accept this fact, often without a rejection of their belief. It is such honesty that accounts for the large number of Christian scholars looking into the origins of their religion.

After listing many examples of contradictions in the Bible, Dr Frederic Kenyon says: "**Besides the larger discrepancies, such as these contradictions, there is scarcely a verse in which there is not some variation of phrase in some copies (of ancient manuscripts from which the Bible has been collected). No one can say that those additions or omissions or alterations are matters of mere indifference.**" [65]

It is in the preface of the *Revised Standard Version* of the Bible, 1978, that thirty-two Christian scholars "**of the highest eminence,**" backed by **fifty Christian denominations,** wrote of the authorized version, also known as the *King James Version*, that: "**The King James Version has grave defects, so many and so serious as to call for revision.**"

In 1957, the *Jehovah's Witnesses* published the headline *"50,000 errors in the Bible"* in their *AWAKE* magazine writing: "There are probably 50,000

---

[64] The Book of Jeremiah 8: 8-9
[65] Frederic Kenyon, Our Bible and the Ancient Manuscripts

errors in the Bible, errors which have crept into the Bible text."[66] Nevertheless, they go on to say, "as a whole the Bible is still accurate." ?!

In *The Story of the Manuscripts*, the Reverend George E. Mernil quotes Professor Arnold as stating: "There are not more than 1500 to 2000 places in which there is any uncertainty whatever as to the true text."

The *Five Gospels* written by the *'Jesus Seminar,'* a group of **seventy four renowned Christian scholars from biblical studies institutes and universities all over the world,**[67] was the result of six years of dedicated study.

Deciding to produce a translation of the gospels which would not be biased by their personal Christian faith, they endeavoured to discover the true words of Jesus in the Bible. From the whole text they selected those passages that they believed were the valid sayings of Jesus, and colour-coded them.

Although we have reservations about their elimination of longer passages which ignores the oral cultures' memorization ability, as well as the *Jesus Seminar's* tendency to equate the miraculous with myth, their conclusion was that: **"82% of the words ascribed to Jesus in the gospels were not actually spoken by him."** [68]

They go on to say: **"Biblical scholars and theologians alike have learned to distinguish the Jesus of history from the Christ of faith. It has been a painful lesson for both the church and scholarship. The distinction between the two figures is the difference between a historical person who lived in a particular time and place and a figure who has been assigned a mythical role, in which he descends from heaven to rescue mankind and, of course, eventually return there."**

---

[66] 8th September 1957

[67] Jesus Seminar, Robert W. Funk and Roy W. Hoover (translators and eds.), *The Five Gospels* (1993), pp.533-537

[68] ibid. p.5

The quotes above are merely the authors' opinions, the second quote about the mythical role can be understood from the fact that the concept of Jesus in Christianity is largely based on pagan Roman mythical characters and this will be addressed in a following chapter.

From the *Jesus Seminar* is an archaeological fact that is far more important than what can be regarded as 'their opinion': "In fact we do not have original copies of any of the gospels. We do not possess autographs of any of the books of the entire Bible. The oldest surviving copies of the gospels date from about 175 years after the death of Jesus, and no two copies are precisely alike. And handmade manuscripts have almost always been "corrected" here and there, often by more than one hand. Further, this gap of almost two centuries means that the original Greek (or Aramaic) text was copied more than once, by hand before reaching the stage in which it has come down to us." [69]

"The oldest copies of any substantial potion of the Greek gospels still in existence – so far as we know – date to about 200 C.E. However, a tiny fragment of the Gospel of John can be dated to approximately 125 C.E. or earlier, the same approximate date as the fragments of the Egerton Gospel (Egerton is the name of the donor). But these fragments are too small to afford more than tiny apertures onto the history of the text. Most of the important copies of the Greek gospels have been "unearthed" – mostly in museums, monasteries, and church archives – in the 19th and 20th centuries." [70]

They finally sum up this issue by saying: "...the stark truth is that the history of the Greek gospels, from their creation in the first century until the discovery of the first copies at the beginning of the third century, remains largely unknown and therefore unmapped territory."

---

[69] ibid. p.6
[70] ibid. p.9

Peake's Commentary of the Bible notes: "It is well known that the primitive Christian Gospel was initially transmitted by word of mouth and that this oral tradition resulted in variant reporting of word and deed. It is equally true that when the Christian record was committed to writing, it continued to be the subject of verbal variation, involuntary and intentional, at the hands of scribes and editors." [71]

Encyclopedia Brittanica highlights: "Yet, as a matter of fact, every book of the New Testament, with the exception of the four great Epistles of St. Paul is at present more or less the subject of controversy and interpolations (inserted verses) are asserted even in these." [72]

After listing many examples of contradictory statements in the Bible, Dr Frederic Kenyon states: "Besides the larger discrepancies, such as these, there is scarcely a verse in which there is not some variation of phrase in some copies (of the ancient manuscripts from which the Bible has been collected). No one can say that these additions or omissions or alterations are matters of mere indifference." [73]

Ehrman mentions: "In any event, none of the original manuscripts of the books of the Bible now survive. What *do* survive are copies made over the course of centuries, or more accurately, copies of the copies of the copies, some 5366 of them in the Greek language alone, that date from the second century down to the sixteenth. Strikingly, with the exception of the smallest fragments, no two of these copies are exact. No one knows how many different, or variant readings, occur among the surviving witnesses, but they must number in the hundreds of thousands." [74]

---

[71] Peake's Commentary on the Bible, p.633
[72] Encyclopedia Brittanica, 12th Edition, Vol. 3, p.643
[73] Kenyon, Eyre and Spottiswoode, *Our Bible and the Ancient Manuscripts*, p.3
[74] Bart Ehrman, The Orthodox Corruption of Scripture, p.27

Toland observes: "We know already to what degree, imposture and credulity went hand in hand in the primitive times of the Christian Church, the last being as ready to receive as the first was ready to forge books. This evil grew afterwards not only greater when the Monks were the sole transcribers and the sole keepers of all books good or bad, **but in the process of time it became almost absolutely impossible to distinguish history from fable, or truth from error as to the beginning and original monuments of Christianity.** How immediate successors of the Apostles could so grossly confound the genuine teaching of their masters with such as were falsely attributed to them? Or since they were in the dark about these matters so early, how came such as followed them by a better light? And observing that such Apocryphal books were often put upon the same footing with the canonical books by the Fathers. I propose these two questions: **Why should all the books cited genuine by Clement of Alexander, Origen, Tertullian and the rest of such writers not be accounted equally authentic?** And what stress should be laid on the testimony of those Fathers who not only contradict one another but are also often inconsistent with themselves in their relations of the very same facts?" [75]

Ehrman states further that: "**Nonetheless, there are some kinds of textual changes for which it is difficult to account apart from the deliberate activity of a transcriber. When a scribe appended an additional twelve verses to the end of the Gospel of Mark, this can scarcely be attributed to mere oversight.**" [76]

Peake's Commentary on the Bible: "**It is now generally agreed that 9-20 are not an original part of Mark. They are not found in the oldest Manuscript, and indeed were apparently not in the copies used by Matthew and Luke.** A 10th century Armenian Manuscript ascribes the passage to Aristion, the Presbyter mentioned by Papias (ap.Eus. HE III, xxxix, 15)."

---

[75] John Toland, *The Nazarenes* (1718), p.73
[76] The Orthodox Corruption o Scripture, pp.27-28

Kenyon et al note that: "Indeed an Armenian translation of St. Mark has quite recently been discovered, in which the last twelve verses of St. Mark are ascribed to Aristion, who is otherwise known as one of the earliest of the Christian Fathers; and it is quite possible that this tradition is correct."[77]

M.A. Yusseff observes: "As it happens, **Victor Tununensis, a sixth century African Bishop related in his Chronicle (566 AD) that when Messala was consul at Constantinople (506 AD), he "censured and corrected" the Gentile Gospels written by persons considered illiterate by the Emperor Anastasius. The implication was that they were altered to conform to sixth century Christianity of previous centuries.**" [78]

Godfrey Higgins: "It is impossible to deny that the Benedictine Monks of St. Maur, as far as Latin and Greek language went, were very learned and talented. In Cleland's *Life of Lanfranc – Archbishop of Canterbury*, is the following passage: "Lanfranc, a Benedictine Monk, Archbishop of Canterbury, having found the Scriptures much corrupted by copyists, applied himself to correct them, as also the writings of the fathers, agreeably to the orthodox faith, *Secundum Fidem Orthodxum*"." [79]

Higgins goes on to say: "The same Protestant divine has this remarkable passage: "Impartially exacts from me the confession, that **the orthodox have in some places altered the Gospels...(the New Testament) in many passages has undergone such serious modification of meaning as to leave us in painful uncertainty as to what the Apostles had actually written.**" [80]

---

[77] Our Bible and the Ancient Manuscripts, pp.7-8

[78] M.A. Yusseff, The Dead Sea Scrolls, the Gospel of Barnabas and the New Testament, p.81

[79] Sir Godfrey Higgins, History of the

[80] James Bentley, *Secrets of Mount Sinai*, p.117

In all, Tischendorf uncovered over 14,800 "corrections" to just one ancient manuscript of the Bible, the *Codex Sinaiticus* (one of the two most ancient copies of the Bible available to Christianity today), by nine (some say ten) separate "correctors," which had been applied to this one manuscript over a period from 400 C.E. to about 1200 C.E.

Tischendorf strove in his dealings with the texts to be as honest and as humanly possible. For this reason he could not understand how the scribes could have so continuously and so callously "allowed themselves to bring in here and there changes, which were not simple verbal changes, but materially affected the meaning," or why they "did not shrink from cutting out a passage or inserting one."

In the preface of the *New Revised Standard Version of the Bible*[81] we read: "**Yet the King James Version has serious defects. By the middle of the nineteenth century, the development of biblical studies and the discovery of many biblical studies and the discovery of many biblical studies and the discovery of many biblical manuscripts more ancient than those on which the King James Version was based, made it apparent that these defects were so many as to call for revision.**"

In the introduction to the same 'version' they say: "**Occasionally it is evident that the text has suffered in the transmission and that none of the versions provides a satisfactory restoration. Here we can only follow the best judgement of competent scholars as to the most probable reconstruction of the original text.**" [82]

The great luminary of Western literature, Edward Gibbon, explains the tampering of the Bible with the following words: "Of all the manuscripts now extant, above fourscore in number, some of which are more than 1200 years old, the orthodox copies of the Vatican, of the Complutensian editors,

---

[81] Oxford Press

[82] Here then we observe that even in the introductions to copies of the Bible, learned Christians are actually admitting that the transmission of the Bible is not trustworthy!!

of Robert Stephens are becoming invisible; and the two manuscripts of Dublin and Berlin are unworthy to form an exception. In the eleventh and twelfth centuries C.E. the Bibles were corrected by Lanfranc, Archbishop of Canterbury, and by Nicholas, a Cardinal and librarian of the Roman Church, *Secundum Orthoxum Fidem*. Not withstanding these corrections, the passage is still wanting in twenty five Latin manuscripts, the oldest and fairest; two qualities seldom united, except in manuscripts. The three witnesses have been established in our Greek Testaments by the prudence of Erasmus; the honest bigotry of the Complutensian editors; the typographical fraud, or error, of Robert Stephens in the placing of a Crotchet and the deliberate falsehood, or strange misapprehension of Theodore Beza." [83]

Thiede's First Century Fragments

There are some who claim to hold early Christian texts, notably the German scholar, Carsten Thiede. Thiede claimed to have discovered three papyrus fragments of Matthew's Gospel from the first century, one hundred years earlier than previously thought. Thus, these fragments could be viewed as 'eye-witness' accounts of the life of Jesus. This opinion was popular with Evangelical Christians such as Joseph 'Jay' Smith, who relies heavily on Thiede's work.

Graham Stanton one of Britain's most eminent New Testament scholars and a leading specialist on Matthew's Gospel refuted the claims of Thiede. **Criticism was also gathered from ten other prominent scholars in the field.** The following, along with Stanton, also refute the erroneous claim made by Thiede that a fragment of Mark's Gospel has been found amongst the *Dead Sea Scrolls*: Professor Hartmut Stegemann, a leading Qumran specialist who teaches at the *University of Göttingen*; Professor Hans-Udo Rosenbaum of the *University of Münster*; Dr R.G. Jenkins of Melbourne and Dr Timothy Lim, the Qumran specialist from Edinburgh.[84]

---

[83] Edward Gibbon, Decline and Fall of the Roman Empire, Volume 4, p.418
[84] Graham Stanton, *Gospel Truth* (1997) pp.200-202

Thiede's extremely radical claims were discredited by the Jewish scholar Hershel Shanks in the May/June 1997 issue of *Biblical Archaeological Review* and Thiede's work was also referred to in the same journal as *"Junk Scholarship."* [85]

Professor Keith Elliot of the *University of Leeds* published a very critical review of *The Jesus Papyrus*, Thiede's book, in *Novum Testamentum*, a leading journal which publishes specialist articles on the New Testament writings and related topics. January 1997 saw the publication of T.C. Skeat's research, *The Oldest Manuscript of the Four Gospels*, in *New Testament Studies*, another important academic journal. Recognised as a leading specialist on Greek manuscripts for sixty years, Skeat shows that beyond reasonable doubt, the fragments of Matthew and Luke belonged to the earliest surviving four gospel codex. On page 30 of his research, Skeat says: "If I say that I prefer to keep Robert's late second century dating, it is because I feel that circa 200 C.E. gives an unwarranted air of precision."

Stanton's own research on the origin and theological significance of the fourfold gospel was published in *New Testament Studies* in July 1997.[86] He mentions that the earliest Christian writer who seems to have known and used four gospels is Justin Martyr who wrote his *Apology* and his *Dialogue* shortly after the middle of the second century. Stanton says: **"There is no earlier evidence…in the period shortly before 150 AD Christians began to include the four gospels in one Codex.** This practice encouraged acceptance of the fourfold Gospel, i.e. the conviction that the four gospels – no more, no less – are the Church's foundation writings." [87]

Stanton also stipulates that his conclusion is somewhat more cautious than the generally accepted view that the fourfold gospels were an innovation when Irenaeus wrote in about 180 C.E. Other important studies that have ruled out Thiede's claims include:

---

[85] Biblical Archaeological Review (January/February 1997)
[86] *New Testament Studies*, Vol. 43 (July 1997), pp.317-346
[87] Gospel Truth, p.197

1. Dr Klaus Wachel's work published in *Zeitschrift für Papyrologie und Epigraphik* [88]

2. Peter M. Head in *'The Date of the Magdalen Papyrus of Matthew – A Response to C.P. Theide.'* [89]

3. D.C. Parker in *'Was Matthew Written Before 50 C.E.? – The Magdalen Papyrus of Matthew.'* [90]

4. In a special issue devoted to the Gospels, the popular German news magazine, *Der Spiegal*, noted in May 1996 that a famous contemporary papyrologist, Peter Parsons, Regius Professor of Greek at Oxford University, has also presented evidence that flies in the face of Carston Thiede's hypothesis.

Translation of the Bible

We would like to bring the reader's attention to the scholar William Tyndale and his students who were persecuted and branded as heretics by the established Church in the 16th century for merely translating the Bible into the English language for the benefit of the masses of English people who could not read Latin. (!?)

Up until this time, it was illegal for the "layman" to even look at the Bible, one had to be a fully qualified priest or clergyman!? So it actually took the established Church which claims today to be for all of humanity, 1600 years before they realised that the Bible (the so called 'word of God') should be made accessible in other languages!

Tyndale is sometimes referred to as the *"Father of the English Bible,"* he was born in Gloucestershire and educated at Oxford (B.A. in 1512 and an M.A. in 1515) and at Cambridge where he studied Greek. Tyndale's translation,

---

[88] Vol. 107, (1995) pp.73-80
[89] In *Tyndale Bulletin*, Vol. 46 (1995), pp.251-285
[90] *Expository Times*, Vol. 107 (1995), pp. 40-43

which was done in exile in Germany, was the first printed New Testament in English translated from Greek. Cuthbert Tunstall, Bishop of London at the time, bought copies of Tyndale's translation in huge numbers in order for them to be burnt in public. Thomas Moore published a dialogue in which he denounced Tyndale's translation as being **"not worthy to be called 'Christ's Testament,' but rather 'Tyndale's own testament' or the testament of his master – the Antichrist."**

During his time in Antwerp, many attempts were made to lure him back to England. He was arrested by agents of Emperor Charles the 5th and taken to Vilvorde, six miles north of Brussels, where he was imprisoned in a fortress on 21 May 1535.

In August 1536 he was tried, found guilty of heresy (for having the nerve to even translate the Bible!!) and turned over to the secular power for execution. On 6 October 1536, William Tyndale was strangled and burned at the stake.[91] John Wycliff and his students, known as the *Lollards*, also suffered similar persecution for translating the Bible into English.

The evangelical Christians would say that the people who persecuted the two characters, Tyndale and Wycliff, were not "real Christians," yet at the same time the Evangelical Christians denounce and brand as "heretical" the original followers of Jesus who had similar beliefs to Islaam. The lack of tolerance in Christianity is demonstrated in the way it has always treated "heretics" and this kind of demonisation is actually endemic to Christianity of whatever brand. The detailed histories of John Wycliff and William Tyndale can be found in most history books about the Church in England.

---

[91] Bruce Metzger and Michael D. Coogan (eds.), *The Oxford Companion to the Bible* (Oxford University Press: 1993), pp.758-759

Later Christianity and its Parallels in the Wider World

❨When it is said to them: "Follow what Allaah has revealed" they say: "No, rather we will follow that which we found our fathers doing." Even though their fathers understood nothing nor were they guided, they were void of wisdom❩
{*al-Baqarah: 170*}

James H. Baxter, Professor of Ecclesiastical History at *St. Andrews University* says in *Christianity in the Light of Modern Knowledge*: "If Paganism had been destroyed, it was less through annihilation than through absorption. Almost all that was pagan was carried over to survive under a Christian name...local pagan statues were labelled with Jesus' name, transferring him to the cult and mythology associated with the pagan deity."

Will Durant observed: "Christianity did not destroy paganism; it adopted it...From Egypt came the ideas of a divine trinity." [92]

Arthur Findlay in *Rock of Truth* made the point that: "It was not until the year 527 C.E. that it was decided when Jesus was born, and various monks equipped with astrological learning were called in to decide this important point. Ultimately, the Emperor decided that the 25th of December, the date of birth for the pagan Roman god, *Mithra*, be

---

[92]Quoted by M.A.C. Cave, *Is the Trinity Doctrine Divinely Inspired?* (Riyadh: World Assembly of Muslim Youth, 1997), p.25

accepted as the date of birth for Jesus. Up to 680 C.E. no thought had been given to the symbol of Jesus crucified on the cross and prior to that date veneration was accorded to the Mithraic symbol of the lamb. From this time onwards it was ordained that in place of the lamb the figure of a man attached to the cross should be substituted."

Sir James G. Frazier in his famous work *The Golden Bough* noted: "In respect both of doctrines and of rites, the cult of *Mithra* appears to have presented many points of resemblance to Christianity. Taken all together, the coincidences of the Christian with the Heathen festivals are too close and too numerous to be accidental. They mark the compromise which the church in its "hour of triumph" was compelled to make with its vanquished and yet still dangerous rivals."

In Robertson's *Pagan Christs* we read that *Mithra* was believed to be a great mediator between man and God. His birth took place in a cave on December 25th. He was born of a virgin and he travelled far and wide and had twelve disciples (that represent the twelve zodiacal signs). He died in the service of humanity, he was buried but rose again from his tomb and his resurrection was celebrated with great rejoicing. His great festivals were the *Winter Solstice* and the *Equinox* (Christmas and Easter?). He was called the saviour and sometimes figured as a lamb and people initiated themselves into this cult through baptism and sacramental feasts were held in his remembrance.[93] Mithraism was a religion of "salvation." [94]

It is worth noting that in the English language all of the days of the week are actually named after Pagan deities from Northern European cults. For example, *Monday*, is from '*Moon*' as some of the northern European Pagans used to worship the Moon on this day. Thursday is from the Nordic god *Thor*; Friday is from the Nordic god *Freyr*; Saturday is derived from the Roman god *Saturn* and possibly *Saturnalia* which was another Roman

---

[93] Robertson, *Pagan Christs*, p.338
[94] Chambers Compact Reference, *Mythology* (1991), p.132

"celebration" which involved debauchery and inebriation. But the most important pagan naming for a week day is with *Sunday* derived from the Roman sun god *Solis Invictus*, not from *"son of god."* This is why later Christians, accommodating Romans and their culture, hence 'Roman Catholicsim,' worship on 'Sunday,' s-u-n, not s-o-n. The 25ᵗʰ of December was also the birthday of *Sol* and was known as *Natalis Solis Invicti* which was a time of rejoicing, games, public frolics and inducement in slaves. Remember, these same Romans would later preside over the *Council of Nicea*, headed by the Pagan Roman Emperor, Constantine, who was himself considered to be an incarnation and embodiment of the sun god!! *The Council of Nicea* and other "councils" lead to the "official" and "orthodox" doctrines of which books should be placed into the Bible, the trinity and Jesus' date of birth being fixed to the 25ᵗʰ of December.

Edward Gibbon in *The Decline and Fall of the Roman Empire* says: "**The Roman Christians ignorant of his (Jesus') birthday, fixed the solemn festival to the 25ᵗʰ of December, the *Brunalia* or *Winter Solstice*, when Pagans annually celebrated the birthday of *Sol*."** [95]

Groliers Encyclopedia notes: "**Christmas is the feast of the birth of Christ, celebrated on December 25. Despite the beliefs about Christ that the birth stories expressed, the church did not observe a festival for the celebration of the event until the 4ᵗʰ century. Up to this time Rome had celebrated the feats of the *Invincible Sun* on December 25, and even from 274 C.E. under the Emperor Aurelian the feast was still celebrated."**

Sons of God?

In ancient societies there were many people who were referred to as son of god, sons of god, son of the gods and so on. James Dunn, a Trinitarian theologian, summarises the various positions and their contexts: "Those familiar with the wider circles of Hellenistic culture would know that:

---

[95] Edward Gibbon, The Decline and Fall of the Roman Empire; Volume 2, p.383

(1) Some of the legendary *heroes* of Greek (and Roman) myth were called sons of God – in particular, Dionysus and Heracles were sons of Zeus by mortal mothers.

(2) *Oriental rulers*, especially Egyptian, were called sons of god. In particular, the Ptolemies in Egypt laid the claim to the title 'sons of Helios' from the fourth century BC onwards, and at the time of Jesus, 'son of god' was already widely used in reference to Augustus.

(3) *Famous philosophers* also, like Pythagora and Plato, were sometimes spoken of as having been begotten by a god (Apollo).

(4) and in Stoic philosophy Zeus, the supreme being, was though of as father of all men.

(5) Even those whose cultural horizons were more limited to the literature and traditions of Judaism would be aware that 'son of god' could be used in several ways: (5) *angels or heavenly beings*

(6) Regularly of *Israel* or *Israelites*

(7) *The king*, so called only a handful of times in the Old Testament. In intertestimental Judaism these uses of "son of God" were developed.

(8) In 1 Enoch, angels are called "sons of heaven" and "sons of the God of heaven"

(9) Philo in his unique blend of Stoic and Jewish thought calls God "the Supreme Father of Gods and men" and frequently talks of God as Father in relation to the creation, referring to the cosmos as "God's son" and the *Logos* as "God's first born."

(10) Individual Israelites, specifically the righteous man, the Maccabean martyrs or those who do what is good and pleasing to nature.

(11) In particular, attention has recently been drawn to two Jewish charismatics remembered in Rabbinic literature – one Honi, the "circle drawer" (first century C.E.), who according to tradition prayed to God "like a son of the house" and had the reputation of

enjoying a relationship of intimate sonship with God which ensured the success of his petitions...the other Hanina ben Dosa, from the generation following Jesus, who a heavenly voice was said to have addressed as "my son."

(12) Finally, the *Dead Sea Scrolls* have thrown up three interesting fragments: one speaks of the time "when (God?) will have begotten the Messiah among them." In the second, the hoped for Davidic Messiah is described specifically in the language of divine sonship using II Sam 7.11-14...and possibly associating it with Ps. 2.7...the other says of one who apparently is to be a mighty king (Messiah?) – "He shall be hailed as the son of God, and they shall call him Son of the most High...[96]

The degree of similarity between the use of "son of God" with Jewish writings and its use in the wider Hellenistic world is noticeable. In particular, it was obviously a widespread belief or convention that the king was a son of god either as descended from God or as representing God to his people. This is known as *Divine Kingship* and is seen in the tribal cultures of the world. So to both inside and outside Judaism human beings could be called "sons of God" either as somehow sharing the divine mind or as being specially favoured by God or pleasing to God."[97]

Dunn goes on to note: **"The language of divine sonship and divinity was in widespread and varied use in the ancient world and would have been familiar to the contemporaries of Jesus, Paul and John in a wide range of applications."** [98]

---

[96] About this occurrence, Geza Vermes writes: "4Q246 with its intriguing phrases, "son of God" and "son of the Most High," recalling Luke 1, 32, 35, has been the centre of learned and popular speculation for the last twenty years. Four competing theories were proposed before the photograph of the document reached the public." (Vermes, *The Dead Sea Scrolls in English*, 1995)

[97] Dunn, Christology in the Making, p.14-16

[98] ibid. p.17

Isis – Mother of God?

The 'Black Madonnas' of Europe, which can be seen in 7th century C.E. French art, Eastern Europe, Russia, Switzerland and Montserrat, have enormous similarities with Isis.

Isis was an African goddess of Nile Valley civilisations, whose worship eventually diffused to most of the ancient western world. The infant Horus was the begotten son of the resurrected god Osiris and the goddess Isis. The legend of Isis became an ancient international phenomena, Jocelyn Rhys states **"statues of the goddess Isis with the child Horus in her arms were common in Egypt and were exported to all neighbouring and to many remote countries, where they are still to be found with new names attached to them – Christian in Europe, Buddhist in Turkestan, Taoist in China and Japan. Figures of the virgin Isis do duty as representations of Mary, of Hariri, of Juan-Yin, of Kwannon and of other virgin mothers of gods."** [99]

Another interesting fact is that in the pre-Islamic times, the Arabs in Makkah used to worship a goddess called *al-'Uzza*, who was a black woman and her idol was destroyed by the companion of the Prophet Muhammad *(sallallaahu alayhi wassallam)*, Khaalid bin Waleed *(radi Allaahu anhu)*. The pagan Arabs worshiped other goddesses such as *al-Lat* and *al-Manaat*.

In the aspect of 'mother with child,' Isis was pictured as a woman with dark brown skin and this image was dispersed throughout Europe. By the late 3rd century C.E. the cult of Isis worship was the biggest, even over the Roman and Greek goddess cults. [100]

Isis was known as the *"Great Mother,"* the *"Immaculate Virgin,"* *"Our Lady"* and the *"Mother of God."*

[99] Jocelyn Rhys, *Shaken Creeds – The Virgin Birth Doctrine* (1922), pp.115-116 (Chapter 3)

[100] R.E. Witt, *Isis in the Graeco-Roman World* (New York: Cornell University Press, 1971) p.81

During the 4th century C.E. there was discussion in the European Christian Churches concerning the doctrinal status of the Virgin Mary. In 428 C.E., Nestorius patriarch of Constantinople, put forward the belief that he Virgin Mary was a mother to the divine Jesus, differing from the ruling Church faction which insisted that the Virgin Mary was *the* "Mother of God." In 430 C.E. Cyril of Alexandria, called a synod which included the major Christian leaders of Europe. The 431 C.E. official declaration of the Virgin Mary as the "Mother of God" was the result of this synod, known as the *'Council of Ephesus.'* Cyril's faction of the Christian Church formed the European Orthodox Churches, which eventually separated into the Roman Catholic Church and the Eastern Orthodox Church.

The absent Nestorius was ousted from Constantinople and his writings were burned as a result of the *Council of Ephesus*. The attributes and titles which catapulted the Virgin Mary into the realm of goddesshood were borrowed from Isis.[101] Despite the official suppression of the worship of Isis in Europe, it survived in the veneration of the European Black Madonnas, which are the Orthodox Christian images of Mary.

Steven C. Cappannari and Leonard W. Moss state that "the Black Madonnas are powerful images, miracle workers…implored for intercession in the various problems of fertility. Pilgrimages covering hundreds of kilometres are made to shrines of the Black Madonnas…pilgrims journeying to the shrine at Mount Vergine would climb the steps of the Church on their knees, licking each step with their tongues. **The attitude of the pilgrim approaches not reverence but worship.**"[102]

---

[101] Danita Redd, "Black Madonnas of Europe – Diffusion of the African Isis" in Ivan Van Sertima (ed.), African Presence in Early Europe (Transaction Publishers, 1996) p.117

[102] Cappannari and Moss, "Mother Worship – In Quest of the Black Virgin, She is Black Because She is Black" in James J. Preston (ed.), Mother Worship – Theme and Variation (Chapel Hill: University of North Carolina Press, 1982) pp.53-74

The worship of the European Black Madonnas clearly demonstrate the diffusion of the cult of Isis worship into Europe. This diffusion can be investigated through the early development of Byzantine Christian iconography and the adoption by the European Orthodox Christians of various Black goddesses to represent the Virgin Mary.[103]

The Black Madonnas of Europe have a tradition which goes back hundreds of years, before the advent of established Christianity. Isis was the prototype for the black Madonnas of Europe, and was absorbed into the Orthodox Christian Churches of Europe.

Furthermore, Cappannari and Moss state that during the French revolution, engineers destroyed several images of the Virgin Mary. These images and relics were examined and found to be black basalt statues of Isis and Horus. Thus, it is evident that the idols of Europe were converted into statues of Mary.[104]

Similarities with Buddha?

T.W. Doane in his book *Bible Myths and Their Parallels in Other Religions* went as far as dedicating an entire chapter on assessing the comparison between Buddha and later Christian concepts of Jesus as God, God incarnate and "Son of God" etc.

Doane has included a forty-eight point side-by-side narration and detailed analysis from their births until the end of their lives on earth *as recorded in the Bible* and in Buddhist scriptures. Their conception, birth, missions, miracles, temptation, preaching, worship, prophesies, death, ascension, divine-ness, judgment of mankind and many other matters recorded in their orthodox scriptures are almost word for word exact carbon copies of one another. This could also demonstrate that Buddha could have been a Prophet of God, Allaah knows best.

---

[103] Danita Redd

[104] Stephen C. Cappannari and Leonard W. Moss, *"The Black Madonna: An Example of Cultural Borrowing"* in *Scientific Monthly*, (Vol. 73, 1953) pp.319-24

Dr. Muhammad Ansari records the following words from an eminent Christian scholar, S.M. Melamed: "Yet the fact remains, the Buddhist canons were already known to the Western world before the coming of Jesus. Today hardly any Indologist of note denies the organic connection between the two redemptive religions. So close is the connection between them that even the details of the miracles recorded in the "orthodox" scriptures of both religions are the same. It is said that Buddha fed five hundred people with one loaf of bread, that he cured lepers and caused the blind to see."[105]

In 1884 C.E. a German historian of religion by the name of Rudolph Seydel published a very detailed study demonstrating that all of the tales, miracles, their astounding similarities with the much more ancient Buddhist scriptures and accounts.

T.W. Doane observes that even though today Buddha has been elevated to the position of a god, "**there is no reason to believe that Buddha ever claimed to be a higher authority than that of a teacher of religion, but, as in modern factions, there were followers of Buddha after his death who carried out his teachings further than Buddha did himself. These people, not content with praising him during his lifetime, exalted him to the level of a god, and thus within a quarter of a century after his death, Buddha found a place amongst the other deities.**" [106]

---

[105] Islam and Christianity in the Modern World

[106] Due to the popularity and fashionable trend of people in the West entering into Buddhism, as an alternative to the modern consumer industrial complex and its spiritual void, we realise the need to cite some realities of the *"Buddha path."* Even though Buddha never asked people to worship him and never claimed to be the One True God worthy of worship, most Buddhists all over the world worship him and make colossal temples, aesthetic shrines and gigantic statues of "Buddha." Many of the rites of worship involved at such sites include bowing, prostrating and praying, in an attempt to seek help from *"the Buddha."* Meanwhile, most Buddhists will say that they do not worship Buddha and that their way is the "way of true inner peace and

The Word of God

In the Qur'aan, Jesus *(peace be upon him)* is referred to as *'the word,'* as he came into being by the word of Allaah, *"Be"* (Soorah Alee Imraan: 59).

In Christianity however, the adoption of the pre-Christian concept of *'the word'* in the gospel according to John, has been to signify his divinity. The Greek term used in the gospel (John 1:1, 1:14) for *'word'* is *'logos,'* also meaning 'reason' or 'plan.' Thus, Jesus is identified in the gospel with the pagan *logos* of Greek philosophy who was the divine reason implicit in the cosmos, ordering it and giving it form and meaning. In the sixth century C.E. the philosopher Heracletius proposed that there was a *logos* in the cosmic process equivalent to the reasoning power of man.

Philosophers following the teachings of Zeno of Citicum in the third and fourth centuries C.E. known as Stoics, later defined the *logos* as an active, rational and spiritual principle that permeated all reality.

Judaeus Philo of Alexandria, a Greek-speaking Jewish philosopher (d. 45 C.E.) taught that the *logos* was the intermediary between God and the cosmos, being both the agent between God and the cosmos, and both the agent of creation and the agent through which the human mind can comprehend God.[107]

---

spirituality." Even though many young people and Western university students are now getting into Buddhism, with films highlighting the craze such as *Seven Years in Tibet*, Buddhist realities are not really know. For example in the 20th century the Tibetan Buddhists even outlawed the bicycle!? Totally against any kind of progress!

[107] Dr Abu Ameenah Bilal Philips, *The True Message of Jesus Christ* (Dar al-Fatah, 1996) pp.60-61

Where Does This Leave Us?

❨And say: "Truth has now come and falsehood has passed away. Indeed, falsehood, (by its nature) is bound to pass away."❩ *{Soorah 17 al-Israa: 81}*

1.   *Does the Qur'aan have the same problems?*

As we have seen, the Bible suffers from a number of problems. Therefore, being honest and fair, we should also apply similar research criteria in evaluating the authenticity of the Qur'aan. In other words, we will discover what has been written about it and the manuscript evidence of the Qur'aan. However, where we relied upon Christian sources in order to understand the problems of the Bible, we will not rely primarily on Muslim sources to view the Qur'aan as we might then be accused of bias. Nevertheless, we shall quote studies by Muslims and the research of non-Muslim evidence in favour of the Qur'aan and its authenticity. To avoid any bias we shall look at what the majority of non-Muslim scholars have said about the Qur'aan and its authenticity. Firstly, however, let us get a brief history of the Qur'aan and some of the charges that have been made against it.

The Qur'aan was recited by the Prophet Muhammad *(sallallaahua alayhi wassallam)* who, being illiterate himself, used scribes to write down the verses of the Qur'aan on cloth, stones, saddles, date-palm leaves etc. to aid people's memorisation of it. Al-Bukhaaree mentions the following: "When it was revealed,

❨"Not equal are those believers who sit at home and those that strive in the cause of Allaah…"❩   *{an-Nisaa: 95}*

The Prophet *(sallallaahu alayhi wassallam)* said *"Call Zayd ibn Thaabit for me, and tell him to bring the ink-pot and the scapula bone (i.e. paper and pen)."* When Zayd came, the Prophet told him "Write: *"Not equal are those believers who sit at home and those* (to the end of verse)". The parchments on which the Qur'aan was written were so common that Zayd ibn Thaabit reported, *"During the lifetime of the Prophet, we used to compile the Qur'aan from scraps of cloth."* [108]

These written verses were sometimes given to visiting tribes who would take them away to learn. After the death of the Prophet Muhammad *(sallallaahu alayhi wassallam)*, many of the *Huffadh* (those who had memorised the whole of the Qur'aan) were killed at the Battle of Yamamah against the apostates. 'Umar ibn al-Khattaab *(radi Allaahu anhu)* who was the second rightly guided Caliph suggested to the first Caliph, Aboo Bakr as-Siddeeq that they should gather the whole Qur'aan into one written book to keep it safe from being lost. Zayd ibn Thaabit *(radi Allaah anhu)* who was one of the main scribes, took the task of writing down the Qur'aan. Zayd referred to all those who had memorised the Qur'aan and those who had written copies, verifying them with other witnesses. The other companions of the Prophet who helped Zayd to write down and compile the Qur'aan were the four Caliphs themselves as well as 'Ubayy ibn Ka'ab, Abdullaah ibn Mas'ood, Mu'aadh ibn Jabal, Aboo Moosaa al-Ash'aree, Mu'aawiyah ibn Abee Sufyaan, 'Uqba ibn 'Aamir, Abdullaah bin Arqam, Khaalid bin Sa'eed and others, may Allaah be pleased with them.[109]

The Prophet's allowance that the Qur'aan could be recited in seven different Arabic dialects (which is the way the Qur'aan had been revealed) later led to some dissension. Thus Uthmaan, after consultation with other companions, united the Muslims under one reading which was the Quraysh

---

[108] Al-Haakim

[109] For more on this see: M.M. al-Azami, The History of the Qur'anic Text from Revelation to Compilation – A Comparative Study with the Old and New Testaments (Leicester: UK Islamic Academy, 1425 AH/2003 CE), pp.66-76

that the Prophet himself had used. Copies of this Qur'aan were sent to the various parts of the Islamic empire to be used as standard, and all other dialects of reading and writing were ordered to be destroyed.[110]

It should be noted that these books were not burned due to their content, as is sometimes claimed by the Christian missionaries, but rather because people were reciting the Qur'aan in different dialects with slightly different meanings and understandings. Unqualified Christian evangelists sometimes mention the burning of the texts in order to prove that the Qur'aan has suffered from the same changes as the Bible.

The Qur'aan is read by Muslims everyday in their prayers and it is the practice of some Muslims to read the entire Qur'aan in three days, some in a week and many in a month. While it is very easy to memorise, the Qur'aan itself mentions that it is easy to memorise; in many mosques you will find children as young as six that have memorised the whole Qur'aan, or a large section of it, in the pure Arabic language. Comparatively, **this is not found in any other creed, belief, religion, tradition, ideology or theory in the world!** No other follower of any other way can match this memorisation which is itself a stunning miracle and proof of the divine origin of the Qur'aan. No other way of life has children or adults who know their books off by heart. The Qur'aan is considered to be the word of God and is thus given the utmost respect and attention that it deserves, it is not to be compared to mere poetry, myths or stories.

The total agreement throughout the vast Muslim empire upon one standard text of the Qur'aan is one of the strongest arguments for the Qur'aan's authenticity, clearly establishing that it must have been agreed upon from the earliest times. Furthermore, there is next to nothing recorded in history which mention any arguments amongst the Muslims about the Qur'aan and it text. The fact that all the different sects of that arose during the earliest period of Islaam, such as the *Raafidah/Shee'ah*, the

---

[110] For more on this see: Abu Ammaar Yasir Qadhi, *An Introduction to the Sciences of the Qur'aan* (Birmingham: al-Hidaayah, 1420 AH/1999 CE), pp. 135-139

Khawaarij, the *Qadariyyah*, the *Jahmiyyah*, the *Jabriyyah*, the *Murji'ah*, the *Mu'tazila* etc never mentioned in their writings that the Qur'aan was drastically changed. Neither did they come with their own copies of the Qur'aan in order to justify their political or theological viewpoints. This all gives extra weight to the trustworthy nature of the Qur'aan. All of these sects had to quote from the Qur'aan in order to argue their claims, and none of these deviant sects ever claimed that the Qur'aan was inauthentic. The fact that these sects were unable to invent or add a single verse to the Qur'aan proves that the Muslims were unanimously united upon a single text of the Qur'aan from the earliest periods of Islamic history.[111]

2.   Manuscript Evidence of the Qur'aan

The first point to note is that the absence of manuscripts does not prove that the Qur'aan in the hands of the Muslims is not the Qur'aan that was revealed to the Prophet Muhammad.

Secondly, the existence of early documentary evidence does not actually prove that these were the words spoken or received by Muhammad, or indeed any other historical character. Although this is something that the Western historian would like, or demand, it is in fact not necessarily that reliable. The Muslims of the earliest generations, including that of the Prophet, indeed the Prophet Muhammad himself, considered writing as a useful tool, both of preservation and reference, but it has never been accepted as sufficient in and of itself.

---

[111] The idea that the Qur'aan has been changed has only emerged during the modern era. Heretical sects of *Shee'ah* for example have claimed that the Qur'aan was changed by the *Sahaabah*. A *Shee'ah* writer called at-Tabarsee wrote *Fasl al-Khitaab* in which he compiled the quotes of modern *Shee'ah* scholars who had claimed that the Qur'aan has been changed.   Also the non-Muslim sect of the *Ahmadiyyah/Qadiyaanis*, the sect founded by the Indian heretic and non-Muslim, Ghulam Ahmad in the 19th century, also have their own Qur'aan in which they have twisted verses of the Qur'aan due to their ignorance of the Arabic language

An example of this is when Umar ibn al-Khattaab was approached by some of the Jews from Khaybar claiming that they had a document from the Prophet Muhammad guaranteeing their right to stay. Umar rejected it, claiming it to be a fake on the basis that it contradicted what was orally transmitted from the Prophet himself on the issue. This highlights three issues of benefit to this discussion. First, the possibility of forgery of a document; secondly, the benefit and need for a sound chain of oral transmission and thirdly that hostile parties certainly do not formulate a more reliable source of information.

3. Early Qur'aanic Manuscripts in Our Possession

Most of the early original Qur'aan manuscripts with us now date from after the 2nd century. There *are* however a number of odd fragments of Qur'aanic papyri which date from the first century as mentioned in *Die Entstehun des Qur'an*. There is also a complete Qur'aan in the *Egyptian National Library* on parchment made from gazelle skin which has been dated 68AH. This copy has also been mentioned by Von Dennfer.[112]

Narrations differ as to how many copies were directly ordered and sent out by the Caliph 'Uthmaan, but they range from four to seven. It seems certain from various Muslim historical sources that several were lost, through fire amongst other things. There are four copies that are attributed to 'Uthmaan.

The Tashkent Manuscript

It seems that the copy in Tashkent also known as the Samarqand manuscript may be the same copy of the Qur'aan which Uthmaan kept for himself and was killed while reading it. A book entitled *Tarikh al-Mushaf al-Uthman fee Tashkent* by Makhdoon gives a number of reasons for the authenticity of the manuscript:

---

[112] Ahmed Von Dennfer, *Ulum al-Qur'an* (Islamic Foundation, 1983)

1. The *mus-haf* is written in a script used in the first fifty years of *Hijrah*

2. It is written on parchment made from gazelle

3. There are no diacritical marks which is indicative of early manuscripts.

4. It does not have the vowelling marks which were introduced by Abu'l-Aswad ad-Du'alee who died in 68 AH, suggesting that it is earlier than this.

Abdur-Rahmaan Lomax has noted in his *Authenticity of the Qur'an*, that the parchment leaves of the Tashkent Qur'aan were judged by A. Shebunin[113] to have been written *"not later than at the beginning of the second century AH."* So even if it this manuscript is not one of the Uthmanic Qur'aans it is still very early indeed.

Objections to the Tashkent document concerning the presence of illuminations between the *Soorahs*, may be addressed, not necessarily meaning that it is not the Uthmanic manuscript. It is possible that the medallions were used from an early time, or that they were added at a later date. Similarly, the irregularity of the codex also suggests two possibilities. Firstly, as suggested by Lomax, the manuscripts may have been repaired as the pages disintegrated. The second possibility is that the document was originally written by several different scribes. The difference between the Samarqand and Tashkent manuscripts in terms of the number of lines per page etc are not arguments that in any way disprove the early dating of these manuscripts or their attribution to the scribes working under Zayd bin Thaabit.

---

[113] A Russian scholar whose report on the Tashkent manuscript formed the basis of Issac Mendelsohn's report on the same text called *The Columbia University Copy of the Samarqand Kufi Qur'an*, (*The Moslem World* in *A Christian Quaterly*, Vol.30, 1940)

The Kufic Script

Many of the Christian missionaries and evangelists assert that the Qur'aan is not in *Kufic* script, therefore a concise analysis of this claim is necessary.

The 'Uthmaanic Qur'aans were written in this script and it is almost incomprehensible to modern-day Arabic readers. The script was written without *hamzahs*, *nuqaat* (dots) or *tashkeel* (vowel marks). This was the manner of writing at that time. Therefore, a straight line could represent the letter *baa*, *taa*, *thaa* or *yaa*. It was only by context that the appropriate letters and vowels could be differentiated. The Arabs at that time were accustomed to such a script and would thus substitute the appropriate letter and vowel depending on the context.[114]

A Muslim scholar, al-Qalqashandi, maintains that *Kufic* script is said to have been the earliest script from which the other scripts developed. He writes, **"The Arabic script (*Khatt*) is the one which is now known as *Kufic*. From it evolved all the present pens."** [115]

The terms that came to be applied to these scripts by the early Arabs could not have the chronological significance that some later Arabs and most Western writers have put to them. For is it the case that the name of a thing (i.e *Kufic*) necessarily indicates its ultimate origin? The fact is that the script which later came to be known as *"Kufic"* has its origin far earlier than the founding of the city of Kufa. Atiq Siddiqui writes: **"The *Kufic* or angular variety of the Arabic script, has been traced about a hundred years before the foundation of the town Kufa, 638C.E. (17 A.H.) to which place the style owes its name."** [116]

That is to say, the city was founded in 17 A.H. and the *Kufic* style originated a hundred years before that time! Importantly, this disagrees with many of the Christian missionary theories such as that of Joseph 'Jay'

---

[114] An Introduction to the Sciences of the Qur'aan, p.141
[115] *Kitaab ul-A'sha* (Vol. 3, p.15)
[116] The Story of Islamic Calligraphy, p.9

Smith. This conclusion is agreed upon by other writers, we read in *The Splendour of Islamic Calligraphy*: "However, the *Kufic* script cannot have originated in Kufa, since that city was founded in 17 AH/638 C.E. and the *Kufic* script is known to have existed before that date."[117]

The arbitrary dating of the origins of this script by those who attempt to disregard Islamic documentary evidence also contradicts early coin and rock inscriptions which have been commented upon by Western writers. Regarding the tombstone of 'Abdur-Rahmaan ibn Khayr al-Hajaree, 31 A.H. Nabia Abbott writes: "The earliest inscription, the tombstone of 'Abdur-Rahmaan ibn Khayr al-Hajari, dated 31/652...it is certainly not Makkan and can safely be considered as poor *Kufic*."[118]

Welch dates a milestone as pre-93 A.H. from the time of the Caliph Abdul-Maalik, who reigned from 685 -705 CE, written in *Kufic* script.[119]

An Umayyad coin, minted in Damascus, inscribed in early *Kufic* script, is dated at 107 AH. Its inscription reads: *"There is none worthy of worship but Allaah, He is One and has no partner."*[120]

Another Umayyad coin, minted in Wasit, Iraaq, inscribed in the early *Kufic* script is dated at 108 AH, as can be seen in Room 34 of the British Museum. The inscription reads: *"There is none worthy of worship but Allaah, He is One and has no partner."*

The Topkapi Manuscript
Concerning the Topkapi manuscript there is an interesting clause in the *Treaty of Versailles (Article 246)*: "Within six months from the coming into force of the present treaty, Germany will restore to his majesty King of Hijaz, the original Qur'an of Caliph Uthman."

---

[117] Sijelmasi and Khatibi, p.97
[118] Abbott, Rise and Development, p.19
[119] Welch, Calligraphy in the Arts of the Muslim World, p.44
[120] British Museum, Room 34

It is suggested that this manuscript is dated just after the first century after Hijrah. Dr Muhammad Shaybaanee considered it as Uthmanic, Muhammad Hamidullaah also agreed.

The Islamic Museum of Istanbul

This does not seem to be an original Uthmanic manuscript, but the oldest copy from the original. It is written in *Makki* script and can almost certainly be dated to before the end of the first Islamic century.

Husayn Mosque in Cairo

This is the oldest of all manuscripts, and is either original or an exact copy from the original with similarity to the *Madini* script. It is attributed to Ali Ibn Abee Taalib and is written in early *Kufic* script which Ali would have used and may even be Ali's own handwriting, Allaah knows best.

Other Qur'aanic Manuscripts

There are also other Qur'aans attributed to Ali, Ibn Nadim and Ibn Ayn Aba claim that Ali wrote three Qur'aans of which there is one in *Daar al-Qutb*, Najaf. It has written on it, "**Ali Ibn Abee Taalib wrote it in the year 40 AH.**"

There are Qur'aanic manuscripts attributed to Hajjaaj ibn Mu'awiyah dated 49 AH and Uqba ibn Amir dated 52 AH in Turkey. More information on this topic can be found in *Tareekh al-Khatim al-Arabi* or Dr Salahuddeen al-Munajjid. There are many other Qur'anic manuscripts from the first century of Islaam, we have only cited the most famous, al-Azami relying on the work of 'Awwaad made a list of twenty seven *Mushafs* that included the manuscripts we have just mentioned here.[121]

It is also worth noting that there is no deviation in these manuscripts from the Qur'aan in our possession today. The *Institute fur Koranforschung, University of Munich*, Germany, had collected and collated some 42,000 complete or incomplete copies of the Qur'aan, gathered from all over the

---

[121] M.M. al-Azami, pp.319-318

world. After some fifty years of study they reported that in terms of differences between the various copies there were no variants, except occasional mistakes of copyists which could easily be ascertained. The institute was destroyed by American bombs during the Second World War.

4.   *What do non-Muslim scholars say about the Qur'aan?*

We would like to mention what recognised non-Muslim scholars of Islaam have said about the Qur'aan. These are scholars who are not of the same ilk as the radical fringe minority of de-mythologiser Orientalists. A brief examination into a few statements from some of these writers would be indicative of the dominant opinion on the issue and of its divine nature:

a.   Adrian Brockett – "The transmission of the Qur'aan after the death of Muhammad was essentially static, rather than organic. There was a single text, and nothing significant, not even allegedly abrogate material, could be taken out nor could anything be put in. this applied even to the early Caliphs. **The efforts of those scholars who attempt to reconstruct any other hypothetical original versions of the (written) text are therefore shown to be disregarding half the essence of Muslim scripture.**"[122]

b.   Arthur J Arberry – "Apart from certain orthological modifications of the originally somewhat primitive method of writing, intended to render unambiguous and easy the task of reading and recitation, **the Qur'an as printed in the twentieth century is identical with the Qur'an as authorised by Uthman more than 1300 years ago.**"[123]

---

[122] Approaches to the History of the Interpretation of the Qur'an, p.44

[123] From his introduction to his translation of the Qur'aan

c. John B. Taylor – "Thus we feel confident that the Qur'an which we have today is, as far as is humanly possible, **the text which was established within a few years of the Prophet's death.**"[124]

d. Harry Gaylord Dorman – "It is a literal revelation of God, dictated to Muhammad by Gabriel, perfect in every letter. It is an ever-present miracle witnessing to itself and to Muhammad, the Prophet of God. Its miraculous quality resides partly in style, so perfect and lofty that neither men nor jinn could produce a single chapter to compare with its briefest chapter, and partly in its content of teachings, prophecies of the future, and amazingly accurate information such as the illiterate Muhammad could never have gathered of his own accord."[125]

e. Laura Veccia Vaglieri – "On the whole we find in it a collection of wisdom which can be adopted by the most intelligent of men, the greatest of philosophers and the most skilful of politicians...**But there is another proof of the divinity of the Qur'an; it is the fact that is has been preserved intact through the ages since the time of its revelation till the present day...** Read and re-read by the Muslim world, this book does not rouse in the faithful any weariness; it rather, through repetition, is more loved every day. It gives rise to a profound feeling of awe and respect in the one who reads it or listens to it."[126]

f. H.A.R. Gibb – "**Well then, if the Koran were his own (Muhammad's) composition other men could rival it. Let them produce ten verses like it. If they could not (and it is obvious that they could not), then let them accept the Koran as an outstanding evidential miracle.**"[127]

---

[124] Thinking About Islam
[125] Towards Understanding Islam (New York: 1948), p.3
[126] Apologie de l'Islamisme, pp.57-59
[127] *Mohammedanism* (OUP), p.42

g. G. Margoliouth – "The Koran admittedly occupies an important position among the great religious books of the world. Though the youngest of the epoch-making works belonging to this class of literature, it yields to hardly any in the wonderful effect which it has produced on large masses of men. It has created an all but new phase of human thought and a fresh type of character. It first transformed a number of heterogenous desert tribes of the Arabian peninsula into a nation of heroes, and then proceeded to create the vast politico-religious organisations of the Muhammadan world which are one of the great forces with which Europe and the East have to reckon today."[128]

h. Dr Steingass – "A work, then, which calls forth so powerful and seemingly incompatible emotions even to the distant reader – distant as to time, and still more so as a mental development – a work which not only conquers the repugnance which he may begin its perusal, but changes this adverse feeling into astonishment and admiration, such a work must be a wonderful production of the human mind indeed and a problem of the highest interest to every thoughtful observer of the destinies of mankind; here, therefore, its merits as a literary production should perhaps not be measured by some preconceived maxims of subjective and aesthetic taste, but by the effects which it produced in Muhammad's contemporaries and fellow countrymen. **If it spoke so powerfully and convincingly to the hearts of his hearers as to weld hitherto centrifugal and antagonistic elements into one compact and well-organised body, animated by ideas far beyond those which had until now ruled the Arabian mind, then its eloquence was perfect, simply because it created a civilised nation out of savage tribes, and shot a fresh wolf into the old warp of history.**"[129]

---

[128] J.M. Rodwell, *The Koran* (1977), p.vii

[129] T.P. Hughes, *Dictionary of Islam*, pp. 526-528

i. Arthur J. Arberry – "In making the present attempt to improve on the performance of my predecessors, and to produce something which might be accepted as echoing however faintly the sublime rhetoric of the Arabic Koran, I have been at pains to study the intricate and richly varied rhythms which – apart from the message itself – constitute the Koran's undeniable claim to rank amongst the greatest literary masterpieces of mankind...this very characteristic feature –'that inimitable symphony,' as the believing Pickthall described his Holy Book, "the very sounds of which move men to tears and ecstasy" – has been almost totally ignored by previous translators; it is therefore not surprising that what they have wrought sounds dull and flat indeed in comparison with the splendidly decorated original."[130]

Other non-Muslim scholars who correspond to this position about the Qur'aan include Montgomery Watt, Guilliame, Glubb and Paret. Abdur-Raheem Green noted that, "It is in the disregard of the legacies of these writers that have caused the divergence from the authoritative position by the present radical demythologiser writers[131] and have led to the unanimous rejection of their theories by more balanced critics."[132]

---

[130] The Koran Interpreted (OUP: 1964), p.x

[131] Such as Patricia Crone, Michael Cook, Wansborough, Andrew Rippon, Calder, Yehuda Nevo, G.R. Joseph Puin et al.

[132] Abdur-Raheem Green, An Authoritative Exposition, Part 2 (D) – The Example of the Uninformed, Qur'an VERSION BETA? – Smith and the Qur'an, Manuscript Evidence

Recommended Books and Readings

Dr. Abu Ameenah Bilal Philips:
- *The True Message of Jesus Christ* (Sharjah: Dar al-Fatah: 1997)
- *Did God Become Man?* (Sharjah: Dar al-Fatah, 2003)
- *The Fundamentals of Tawheed* (Birmingham: al-Hidaayah Publishing,)

Dr Asra Rasheed:
- *A Simple Call to One God*
- *Death* (Birmingham: al-Hidaayah Publishing, 2001)

Hamza Mustafa Njozi:
- *The Sources of the Qur'an: A Critical Review of the Authorship Theories* (Riyadh: WAMY, 1991)

Yasir Qadhi:
- *An Introduction to the Sciences of the Qur'aan* (Birmingham: Al-Hidaayah Publishing, 1420 AH/ 1999 CE).

Dr. M.M. al-Azami:
- *The History of The Qur'anic Text from Revelation to Compilation – A Comparative Study with the Old and New Testaments* (Leicester: UK Islamic Academy, 1424 A.H/2003 C.E.)

Website resources:
www.Quran.nu
www.salafimanhaj.com
www.salaf.dk
www.understand-islam.net
www.fatwa-online.com